Alligators

by Derek Zobel

BELLWETHER MEDIA • MINNEAPOLIS, MN

Note to Librarians, Teachers, and Parents:

Blastoff! Readers are carefully developed by literacy experts and combine standards-based content with developmentally appropriate text.

Level 1 provides the most support through repetition of high-frequency words, light text, predictable sentence patterns, and strong visual support.

Level 2 offers early readers a bit more challenge through varied simple sentences, increased text load, and less repetition of high-frequency words.

Level 3 advances early-fluent readers toward fluency through increased text and concept load, less reliance on visuals, longer sentences, and more literary language.

Level 4 builds reading stamina by providing more text per page, increased use of punctuation, greater variation in sentence patterns, and increasingly challenging vocabulary.

Level 5 encourages children to move from "learning to read" to "reading to learn" by providing even more text, varied writing styles, and less familiar topics.

Whichever book is right for your reader, Blastoff! Readers are the perfect books to build confidence and encourage a love of reading that will last a lifetime!

This edition first published in 2012 by Bellwether Media, Inc.

No part of this publication may be reproduced in whole or in part without written permission of the publisher. For information regarding permission, write to Bellwether Media, Inc., Attention: Permissions Department, 5357 Penn Avenue South, Minneapolis, MN 55419.

Library of Congress Cataloging-in-Publication Data
Zobel, Derek, 1983-
Alligators / by Derek Zobel.
   p. cm. – (Blastoff! readers. Animal safari)
Includes bibliographical references and index.
 Summary: "Developed by literacy experts for students in kindergarten through grade three, this book introduces alligators to young readers through leveled text and related photos"–Provided by publisher.
 ISBN 978-1-60014-601-5 (hardcover : alk. paper)
 1. Alligators–Juvenile literature. I. Title.
 QL666.C925Z63 2011
 597.98'4–dc22   2011006236

Printed in the United States of America, North Mankato, MN.
080111   1187

Contents

What Are Alligators?	4
How Alligators Look	6
Land and Water	10
Hunting	14
Glossary	22
To Learn More	23
Index	24

What Are Alligators?

Alligators are large **reptiles**. They live in swamps, marshes, and other **wetlands**.

How Alligators Look

Alligators have long tails. Their tails are half the length of their bodies.

Alligators have between 70 and 80 sharp teeth. They grow new teeth when old ones fall out.

Land and Water

Alligators move slowly on land. They move faster in water.

Alligators **steer** in water with their **webbed feet**. They move their tails back and forth to push forward.

Alligators are powerful **predators**. They hunt turtles, rabbits, and other animals.

Alligators wait near
shore for animals
to come drink.
They hide underwater.

Alligators leap out
of the water
to surprise **prey**.
They grab prey with
their strong **jaws**.

This alligator
has a fish.
CHOMP!

Glossary

jaws—the bones that form the mouths of some animals

predators—animals that hunt other animals for food

prey—animals that are hunted by other animals for food

reptiles—animals that move on their bellies or short legs; reptiles have scales.

steer—to direct movement

webbed feet—feet with thin skin connecting the toes

wetlands—wet, spongy land; bogs, marshes, and swamps are wetlands.

To Learn More

AT THE LIBRARY

Berger, Melvin. *Snap!: A Book About Alligators and Crocodiles.* New York, N.Y.: Scholastic, 2001.

Bredeson, Carmen. *Fun Facts About Alligators.* Berkeley Heights, N.J.: Enslow Elementary, 2008.

Mozelle, Shirley. *Zack's Alligator.* New York, N.Y.: Harper & Row, 1989.

ON THE WEB

Learning more about alligators is as easy as 1, 2, 3.

1. Go to www.factsurfer.com.

2. Enter "alligators" into the search box.

3. Click the "Surf" button and you will see a list of related Web sites.

With factsurfer.com, finding more information is just a click away.

Index

bodies, 6
chomp, 20
drink, 16
fish, 20
grab, 18
grow, 8
hide, 16
hunt, 14
jaws, 18
land, 10
leap, 18
length, 6
marshes, 4
predators, 14
prey, 18
rabbits, 14
reptiles, 4
shore, 16
steer, 12

surprise, 18
swamps, 4
tails, 6, 12
teeth, 8
turtles, 14
underwater, 16
water, 10, 12, 18
webbed feet, 12
wetlands, 4

The images in this book are reproduced through the courtesy of: J & C Sohns / Photolibrary, front cover; Ed Reschke / Photolibrary, p. 5 (top); Tim Mainiero, p. 5 (left); Henry Wilson, pp. 5 (right), 7, 9, 15, (middle); Nancy Nehring, p. 11; Peter Scoones / NPL / Minden Pictures, p. 13; Ron Kimball / Kimballstock, p. 13 (small); Nancy Tripp, p. 15; Z.H. Chen, p. 15 (left); Dewald Kirsten, p. 15 (right); Masa Ushioda / Photolibrary, p. 17; Mark R. Higgins, p. 19; Bob Blanchard, p. 21.